Instant Building Multi-Page Forms with Yii How-to

Learn to create multi-page AJAX enabled forms using Yii

Uday Sawant

PUBLISHING

BIRMINGHAM - MUMBAI

Instant Building Multi-Page Forms with Yii How-to

First published: May 2013

Production Reference: 1160513

Published by Packt Publishing Ltd.
Livery Place
35 Livery Street
Birmingham B3 2PB, UK.

ISBN 978-1-78216-642-9

www.packtpub.com

Credits

Author
Uday Sawant

Reviewer
Sergey Malyshev

Acquisition Editor
Joanne Fitzpatrick

Commissioning Editor
Poonam Jain

Technical Editor
Zafeer Rais

Copy Editor
Aditya Nair

Project Coordinator
Suraj Bist

Proofreader
Maria Gould

Production Coordinator
Melwyn D'sa

Cover Work
Melwyn D'sa

Cover Image
Valentina Dsilva

About the Author

Uday Sawant is a software engineer with a specialization in LAMP stack and cloud computing. He has completed his Master's in Computer Science and has a wealth of experience in infrastructure management and networking. Currently he is working with a startup called Anveshan Technologies as a Sr. Software Engineer.

I would like to thank my parents and my mentor Mr. Mitul Thakkar for helping me write this book.

About the Reviewer

Sergey Malyshev is an IT specialist from Ukraine. He has been working in the IT industry for more than 15 years, eight of which he has devoted to the development of web applications. Out of the conviction that it's impossible to become a great specialist in all areas at the same time, he has chosen for himself PHP, MySQL, and JavaScript as top-priority directions. During his career, Sergey took part in developing dozens of different websites, social networks, CMS, CRM, and ERP systems. He is not only a developer but also an architect, a project manager, and a technical consultant. Apart from his participation in realizing some technical projects, he also organized various advance training courses for IT specialists in the companies where he was employed. As he has a degree in management, Sergey has taken part in the business process automation of companies specializing in software development.

At present, Sergey is working as a software engineer in the company Sugar CRM and deals with the development of one of the most popular customer relationship management systems in the world. Before this he worked on developing applications based on the Yii Framework. Some of them are the search engine for the real estate website `LivingThere.com` and the corporate CMS system WebModulite for the New York design agency Blue Fountain Media. Participation in these projects and also work on his own extension for debugging the Yii application's Yii Debug Toolbar has helped Sergey get vast experience and expert knowledge of the Yii framework.

www.PacktPub.com

Support files, eBooks, discount offers and more

You might want to visit www.PacktPub.com for support files and downloads related to your book.

Did you know that Packt offers eBook versions of every book published, with PDF and ePub files available? You can upgrade to the eBook version at www.PacktPub.com and as a print book customer, you are entitled to a discount on the eBook copy. Get in touch with us at service@packtpub.com for more details.

At www.PacktPub.com, you can also read a collection of free technical articles, sign up for a range of free newsletters and receive exclusive discounts and offers on Packt books and eBooks.

http://PacktLib.PacktPub.com

Do you need instant solutions to your IT questions? PacktLib is Packt's online digital book library. Here, you can access, read and search across Packt's entire library of books.

Why Subscribe?

- ▶ Fully searchable across every book published by Packt
- ▶ Copy and paste, print and bookmark content
- ▶ On demand and accessible via web browser

Free Access for Packt account holders

If you have an account with Packt at www.PacktPub.com, you can use this to access PacktLib today and view nine entirely free books. Simply use your login credentials for immediate access.

Table of Contents

Preface

Instant Building Multi-Page Forms with Yii How-to is a simple and descriptive how-to that provides step-by-step recipes to help you convert your lengthy forms into short, interactive forms. It will show you the inbuilt features of the Yii framework to help you with this tricky task.

What this book covers

Getting started with Yii (Simple) helps you set the Yii environment and create a skeleton of the Yii application.

Connecting to the database (Simple) shows you how to set up a database connection in the Yii application.

Using the Gii tool (Simple) covers the automated code generation features provided by Yii. We will learn how to enable the Gii tool and create Models, CRUD, forms, and application modules.

Creating basic forms (Simple) helps you to create a basic single page form with Yii.

Building multipage forms (Intermediate) shows you how to split your lengthy single page form into multipage forms by validating the form fields and maintaining page data on each page.

Validating forms (Intermediate) gives you details on the form field validation helpers provided by Yii. We will look at various validation helpers, use validation rules provided by Yii, and set our own validation rules.

AJAX forms (Advanced) helps you enable AJAX support for forms. We will take a look at the AJAX helpers provided by Yii, AJAX-based form field validations, and AJAX-based form submission.

Uploading files (Advanced) covers the file upload features provided by Yii. We will look at how to file field validations and restrict uploads to specific file types.

Using multiple models (Intermediate) helps you learn the use of multiple models in a single form.

Customizing looks (Advanced) shows you the options provided by Yii to customize the look of forms. Additionally, we will learn how to create and use skins and customize widgets using the widget factory.

What you need for this book

To use the recipes, tips, and tricks of this book, you need to have the following:

- A web server (any web server with plugins to process PHP scripts)
- PHP version 5.2 + (5.3 recommended)
- A database server (the book has been written with MySQL in mind, but you can easily choose a relational database server of your choice)
- Yii Framework

Who this book is for

This book is great for developers who have a basic understanding of the Yii framework and want to learn about the advanced inbuilt features of Yii. It assumes that the reader has a basic knowledge of PHP development, the working of forms, and AJAX operations.

Conventions

In this book, you will find a number of styles of text that distinguish between different kinds of information. Here are some examples of these styles, and an explanation of their meaning.

Code words in text are shown as follows: " As we need the same form elements in `actionCreate` and `actionUpdate`, Yii has created a single file `_form.php` that contains all the form elements."

A block of code is set as follows:

```
'modules'=>array(
  // uncomment the following to enable the Gii tool
  /*
  'gii'=>array(
    'class'=>'system.gii.GiiModule',
    'password'=>'root',
    // If removed, Gii defaults to localhost only. Edit
carefully to taste.
    'ipFilters'=>array('127.0.0.1','::1'),
  ),  */
),
```

When we wish to draw your attention to a particular part of a code block, the relevant lines or items are set in bold:

```
'modules'=>array(
  // uncomment the following to enable the Gii tool
  /*
  'gii'=>array(
    'class'=>'system.gii.GiiModule',
    'password'=>'root',
    // If removed, Gii defaults to localhost only. Edit
carefully to taste.
    'ipFilters'=>array('127.0.0.1','::1'),
  ), */
),
```

Any command-line input or output is written as follows:

```
yii> framework/yiic  webapp  webRoot/sampleapp
```

New terms and **important words** are shown in bold. Words that you see on the screen, in menus or dialog boxes for example, appear in the text like this: "clicking the **Next** button moves you to the next screen".

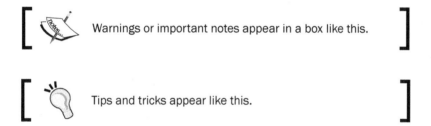

Warnings or important notes appear in a box like this.

Tips and tricks appear like this.

Reader feedback

Feedback from our readers is always welcome. Let us know what you think about this book—what you liked or may have disliked. Reader feedback is important for us to develop titles that you really get the most out of.

To send us general feedback, simply send an e-mail to `feedback@packtpub.com`, and mention the book title via the subject of your message.

If there is a topic that you have expertise in and you are interested in either writing or contributing to a book, see our author guide on `www.packtpub.com/authors`.

Customer support

Now that you are the proud owner of a Packt book, we have a number of things to help you to get the most from your purchase.

Downloading the example code

You can download the example code files for all Packt books you have purchased from your account at `http://www.packtpub.com`. If you purchased this book elsewhere, you can visit `http://www.packtpub.com/support` and register to have the files e-mailed directly to you.

Errata

Although we have taken every care to ensure the accuracy of our content, mistakes do happen. If you find a mistake in one of our books—maybe a mistake in the text or the code—we would be grateful if you would report this to us. By doing so, you can save other readers from frustration and help us improve subsequent versions of this book. If you find any errata, please report them by visiting `http://www.packtpub.com/submit-errata`, selecting your book, clicking on the **errata submission form** link, and entering the details of your errata. Once your errata are verified, your submission will be accepted and the errata will be uploaded on our website, or added to any list of existing errata, under the Errata section of that title. Any existing errata can be viewed by selecting your title from `http://www.packtpub.com/support`.

Piracy

Piracy of copyright material on the Internet is an ongoing problem across all media. At Packt, we take the protection of our copyright and licenses very seriously. If you come across any illegal copies of our works, in any form, on the Internet, please provide us with the location address or website name immediately so that we can pursue a remedy.

Please contact us at `copyright@packtpub.com` with a link to the suspected pirated material.

We appreciate your help in protecting our authors, and our ability to bring you valuable content.

Questions

You can contact us at `questions@packtpub.com` if you are having a problem with any aspect of the book, and we will do our best to address it.

Instant Building Multi-Page Forms with Yii How-to

Welcome to *Instant Building Multi-Page Forms with Yii How-to*. This book is a simple how-to for generating multipage forms with the Yii framework. It covers simple form generation, CRUD generation with the graphical tool Gii, validation of forms, and use of AJAX to validate and submit forms. Additionally, we will use Twitter Bootstrap to change the default look of the forms/pages generated with Yii.

Getting started with Yii (Simple)

We will start with the basic setup of the Yii environment; that is, connecting to a database server and automated generation of Gii and forms with Yii.

Getting ready

This book assumes that you are familiar with the PHP development environment and have a basic development environment set up for PHP application development.

Download the Yii framework from `http://www.yiiframework.com/` and extract its framework folder outside your `Public_html` folder or web root folder. Your application will refer to Yii Bootstrap, `Yii.php`, located inside the `Framework` folder.

How to do it...

Let's move to creating the web application. We will use the command-line utility of Yii to generate the new Yii application.

1. Open the command prompt or a console under Linux.

2. Change the current folder to where the framework has been extracted and enter the following command:

   ```
   yii> framework/yiic  webapp  webRoot/sampleapp
   ```

3. Access the newly generated application at `http://localhost/sampleapp/index.php`.

How it works...

The command will ask you for confirmation and will then generate the basic structure of the Yii application. You can find the details of the directory structure at `http://www.yiiframework.com/wiki/155/the-directory-structure-of-the-yii-project-site/`.

Yii has already created a few simple pages with a **Contact Us** form and a **Login** form. Following is the screenshot of the default **Contact Us** form:

Connecting to the database (Simple)

This recipe describes the steps required to set up database access in a Yii application.

Getting ready

We will use a sample application like the one created in the previous recipe. Additionally, we will need a database server like MySQL, PostgreSQL, or SQLite; also, we will need its credentials and some interface like PHPMyAdmin or command-line access to execute SQL statements against our database.

How to do it...

First of all, we need to create a database.

1. Create a new database in MySQL.
2. Now, go to the sample application and change the folder to `protected/config`. It contains the following three files:
   - `console.php`: This is the configuration file to run applications in console mode
   - `main.php`: This is the configuration file for web applications
   - `test.php`: This is the configuration file for testing web applications
3. Open `main.php` and locate the following code:

```
'db'=>array(
  'connectionString' =>
  'sqlite:'.dirname(__FILE__).'/../data/testdrive.db',
),
// uncomment the following to use a MySQL database
 */
'db'=>array(
  'connectionString' =>
  'mysql:host=localhost;dbname=sampleapp',
  'emulatePrepare' => true,
  'username' => 'root',
  'password' => '',
  'charset' => 'utf8',
),

 */
```

Downloading the example code

You can download the example code files for all Packt books you have purchased from your account at http://www.packtpub.com. If you purchased this book elsewhere, you can visit http://www.packtpub.com/support and register to have the files e-mailed directly to you.

4. The basic application created uses the SQLite database. Remove the code for SQLite configuration and uncomment the MySQL configuration.

5. Change the connectionString, username, and password to match your environment. This is all you need to set the database connection.

There's more...

Yii provides the following three methods to work with database connections:

▸ Active Record

▸ Query Builder

▸ **Data Access Objects (DAO)**

Models in Yii generally extend the CActiveRecord class to provide database access using the Active Record method. This uses a complete object-oriented coding style and creates all the necessary SQL to deal with the database server. Additionally, we can set validation rules in models and also add pre- and post-save hooks. Yii provides the GUI tool named Gii to generate the models for database tables. Though the Active Record method is easy to use, it consumes more memory and needs more execution time than other methods. The sample code to get all records from a table (say, User) will go as follows:

```
$users = User::model()->findAll(array('status'=>'active'));
```

With Query Builder, we create a command object with Yii::app()->db->createCommand() and then add other parts of SQL query with methods such as select, from, where, and join. Query Builder is faster than Active Record and provides a clean API to query the database. For example:

```
$command = Yii::app()->db->createCommand();
$command->select(*)->from('user')->where(array(
'status'=>'active'
));
$users = $command->queryAll();
```

Finally, with a DAO we create the same command as in Query Builder, but instead of adding a query using methods, we pass the entire SQL statement to it as Yii::app()->db->createCommand($sql). This is the fastest method to access the database and also useful when we need to write complex queries such as the following:

```
$sql = 'select * from user where status = "active"';
$users = Yii::app()->db->createCommand($sql)->queryAll();
```

Both Query Builder and the DAO return data in the raw-array format, whereas Active Record returns an array of models with each representing a single row.

Using the Gii tool (Simple)

In this recipe we will take a look at the graphical tool Gii. With the Gii tool, we can generate the following:

► Controller
► CRUD
► Form
► Model
► Module

Getting ready

Set up a Yii environment and create a new web application. Set up the database connection for your database server.

How to do it...

We first need to create a database table.

1. Create a database table user with the following code. This will hold all the necessary information for user registration.

```
CREATE TABLE IF NOT EXISTS 'user' (
  'id' int(11) NOT NULL AUTO_INCREMENT,
  'first_name' varchar(50) NOT NULL,
  'last_name' varchar(50) NOT NULL,
  'gender' enum('male','female') NOT NULL,
  'dob' date NOT NULL,
  'address_1' varchar(255) NOT NULL,
  'address_2' varchar(255) DEFAULT NULL,
  'city' varchar(50) NOT NULL,
  'state' varchar(50) NOT NULL,
  'country' varchar(50) NOT NULL,
  'phone_number_1' varchar(50) NOT NULL,
  'phone_number_2' varchar(50) DEFAULT NULL,
  'email_1' varchar(255) NOT NULL,
  'email_2' varchar(255) DEFAULT NULL,
```

```
'created' timestamp NOT NULL DEFAULT CURRENT_TIMESTAMP
ON UPDATE CURRENT_TIMESTAMP,
'modified' timestamp NOT NULL DEFAULT '0000-00-00
00:00:00',
PRIMARY KEY ('id')
) ENGINE=InnoDB DEFAULT CHARSET=latin1 AUTO_INCREMENT=1 ;
```

2. Next, enable the Gii tool. The Gii tool is related to the database system of our application. So, for security reasons this tool is disabled by default. We need to enable it from `main.php`.

```
'modules'=>array(
    // uncomment the following to enable the Gii tool
    /*
    'gii'=>array(
        'class'=>'system.gii.GiiModule',
        'password'=>'root',
        // If removed, Gii defaults to localhost only. Edit
carefully to taste.
        'ipFilters'=>array('127.0.0.1','::1'),
    ), */
),
```

3. Uncomment the block to enable the Gii tool and set your password in place, and then you are done. The `ipFilters` line is used to restrict the access of the Gii tool to certain IP addresses only; in this case, it's `localhost` (`127.0.0.1 OR ::1`).

4. We need to create models and controllers. To log in to the Gii tool, enter `http://localhost/sampleapp/index.php?r=gii` in your address bar. You will be provided with the login screen. Enter your password to log in.

How it works...

After you log in, you can see all the tasks that can be done with the help of the Gii tool, as shown in the following screenshot:

yii code generator

Welcome to Yii Code Generator!

You may use the following generators to quickly build up your Yii application:

- Controller Generator
- Crud Generator
- Form Generator
- Model Generator
- Module Generator

The tasks shown in the previous screenshot are explained here:

- ▶ **Controller Generator**: It allows you to quickly generate a new controller class with one or more actions and the respective views. The default base class used is `Controller`.

- ▶ **CRUD Generator**: It generates a controller and views that implement CRUD operations for a specified model.

- ▶ **Form Generator**: It can be used to generate a view with form elements for a specified model.

- ▶ **Model Generator**: It generates a model class for a specified database table. The base class used is `CActiveRecord`.

- ▶ **Module Generator**: It provides a base code required by the Yii module

All these generators use the templates under the `gii/generator` folder. You can always customize them or use your own templates to modify the code according to your requirements.

Let's generate a model class for our table user as shown in the following screenshot:

Model Generator

This generator generates a model class for the specified database table.

*Fields with * are required. Click on the highlighted fields to edit them.*

Database Connection *
db (mysql:host=localhost,dbname=sampleapp)

Table Prefix
[empty]

Table Name *
user

Model Class *
User

Base Class *
CActiveRecord

Model Path *
application.models

Build Relations
☑

Code Template *
default (E:\yii\yii-1.1.11\framework\gii\generators\model\templates\default)

[Preview]

Fill in the **Table Name** field and the **Model Class** field will be automatically populated; change it if required. Now click on **Preview**. If the database connection is properly set and Yii finds the table user, it will create the preview of a model file.

Click on the filename to preview the file or click on the **Generate** button to generate the model class. The new class will be stored in the `protected/models` folder.

The model class has some automatically generated functions such as `tableName()`, which returns the name of the table. The function `rules()` is used to specify the validation rules, the function `relations()` is used to specify the relations between two or more model classes, the function `attributeLabels` specifies the names for the attribute/columns in the database table, and the function `search()` sets the criteria for searching through the table data.

In the same way, we can generate the **CRUD** (**Create Retrieve Update Delete**) operations for the model user. Type the name of the model class (`User`) and click on the **Preview** button. A list of files to be created will appear, as shown in the following screenshot:

Code File	Generate ☑
controllers\UserController.php	new ☑
views\user_form.php	new ☑
views\user_search.php	new ☑
views\user_view.php	new ☑
views\user\admin.php	new ☑
views\user\create.php	new ☑
views\user\index.php	new ☑
views\user\update.php	new ☑
views\user\view.php	new ☑

Click on the **Generate** button to generate files. `UserController` will be generated under `protected/controllers` and you can view the files under `protected/view/user`.

The generated controller contains some important functions, such as `accessRules()`, which is used to specify access control (user-level access) for each action in this controller, and `filters()`, which specifies the code to be executed before and/or after action execution. `filters()` can include access-control filters, performance filters, and other user-defined filters.

There's more...

To know more about `filters()`, visit the website `http://www.yiiframework.com/doc/guide/1.1/en/basics.controller#filter`.

Creating basic forms (Simple)

Now we will see the creation and working of basic forms in Yii. We will use the Gii tool to automatically generate CRUD operations and a form.

Getting ready

We will use the table user created in the *Using the Gii tool* recipe. Make sure you have enabled Gii under `config/main.php`.

How to do it...

1. Generate a new model for the table `User`.

2. Generate CRUD operations with the Gii tool as specified in the *Using the Gii tool* recipe.

 As we need to create a simple form, we don't need additional functionality such as admin, index, and update. Feel free to uncheck them when generating CRUD.

How it works...

Yii creates some new files and folders, as follows:

- `protected/models/User.php`: This is a model class file. It deals with database-related tasks such as fetching and storing data, updating, and deleting. The `User` class is extended from the base class `CActiveRecord`.

- `protected/controllers/UserController.php`: This is a controller class extended from the base class `Controller`. This class holds all the code for fetching data using models, data manipulation according to requirements, and sending data to the respective views.

- `protected/views/user`: This folder holds views for all CRUD operations; names starting with _ are partial views that are used in multiple places. The remaining files are views for their respective action names in `UserController.php`.

Let's take a look at the generated `controller` file. Change access rules to enable any user to access our form as follows:

```
return array(
   //allow all users to perform 'index' and 'view' actions
   array('allow',
      'actions'=>array('index','view', 'create'),
      'users'=>array('*'),
   ),
```

All we need to do is add `actionCreate()` to the actions that all users can access.

Now move to `actionCreate()`. This is the action when we access the form with the URL `?r=user/create`. At the first line of `actionCreate`, we instantiate the `User` model. As the `POST` variables are not set, the `if` block is skipped and the form is rendered with the view file `create`, with `model` passed to it as a parameter.

```
public function actionCreate()
{
   $model=new User;
   if(isset($_POST['User']))
   {
      $model->attributes=$_POST['User'];
      if($model->save())
         $this->redirect(array('view','id'=>$model->id));
   }
   $this->render('create',array('model'=>$model));
}
```

In the view of `create.php`, we simply render the partial view with the following lines:

```
<?php echo $this->renderPartial('_form', array(
   'model'=>$model
)); ?>
```

This uses the file `_form.php`, which contains all the form elements and passes to it the model that we received from `actionCreate`. As we need the same form elements in `actionCreate` and `actionUpdate`, Yii has created a single file, `_form.php`, that contains all the form elements. This file is used by both the actions to render the form.

In `_form.php`, we start with creating an instance of the `CActiveForm` widget.

```
<?php $form=$this->beginWidget('CActiveForm', array(
   'id'=>'user-form',
   'enableAjaxValidation'=>false,
)); ?>
```

The HTML code in the following screenshot is created by this widget:

```
<h1>Create User</h1>
▼<div class="form">
  ▼<form id="user-form" action="/others/sampleapp/index.php?r=user/create" method="post">
    ▶<p class="note">…</p>
    ▶<div class="row">…</div>
    ▶<div class="row">…</div>
```

Next we create a space to render error details, if any, with following line:

```
<?php echo $form->errorSummary($model); ?>
```

This adds a DIV element to the page if there are any errors in the form fields.

Next we render all necessary input elements as follows:

```
<div class="row">
  <?php echo $form->labelEx($model,'last_name'); ?>
  <?php echo $form->textField($model,'last_name',array(
    'size'=>50,
    'maxlength'=>50,
  )); ?>
  <?php echo $form->error($model,'last_name'); ?>
</div>
```

The HTML code generated can be seen in the following screenshot:

```
▼<div class="row">
  ▼<label for="User_last_name" class="required">
    "Last Name "
    <span class="required">*</span>
  </label>
  <input size="50" maxlength="50" name="User[last_name]" id="User_last_name" type=
  "text">
</div>
```

The $form->labelEx() method renders the label. It takes the parameter name from the model's attributeLabels function. If no label is set for this attribute, the attribute name is used as the label.

The $form->textField() method renders the actual form field. We use textField for input with the type set to text; dropDownList to select boxes, textArea to render text areas, hiddenField to render hidden fields respectively.

> Look at the name of the input field. It has the format `User[last_name];` this enables us to get all related form fields in a single `User` array, which can be directly assigned to the models' attributes with a single line of code, `$model->attributes = $_POST['User']`, thereby reducing the number of lines of code.

The `$form->error()` method adds error messages in a separate `div` element if there is any error with the data in this field.

Finally, we have added a submit button with the echo `CHtml::submitButton('Create')`. It creates an input element with type set to `submit` and is attached to the parent form by default. We can end the form widget with `$this->endWidget();`.

When the user clicks on the create button, the form data is submitted to the same `actionCreate` function as POST data.

Now as the `$_POST['User']` field is set, the code enters the `if` block. We assign all attributes marked as `safe` in the `User` variable of type POST to model with `$model->attributes = $_POST['User']`. This is called Mass Assignment.

Then on the next line, we save the model with `$model->save()`. The method `save()` internally validates the model to check if the user has entered the valid data. Here, the rules specified in the method rules under the `User` model are used to validate the form data.

```
public function rules()
{
  return array(
    array(
      'first_name, last_name, gender, dob, address_1,
      city, state, country, phone_number_1, email_1,
      created', 'required'
    ),
    array(
      'first_name, last_name, city, state, country,
       phone_number_1, phone_number_2',
       'length', 'max'=>50
    ),
    array('gender', 'length', 'max'=>6),
    array(
      'address_1, address_2, email_1, email_2',
      'length', 'max'=>255
    ),
    array('modified, dob', 'safe'),
    array(
      'id, first_name, last_name, gender, dob, address_1,
```

```
        address_2, city, state, country, phone_number_1,
        phone_number_2, email_1, email_2, created,
        modified', 'safe', 'on'=>'search'
    ),
  );
}
```

In the first array, we specify all the required fields; in the next three arrays, we set the maximum length of data for each field. In the fourth array, additionally, we mark the attributes `dob` and `modified` as `safe`. We also make several attributes as `safe` when the scenario is set to `search`.

If the validation is successful, the form data is persisted to the database and the page is redirected to the action `view`, which displays all the captured data.

If the validation fails, the same model is passed to the view but now with the respective validation errors set in it. The line `$form->errorSummary($model)` renders the summary of all errors in the form and the line `$form->error()` adds the error line below the respective fields.

There's more...

We have seen the automated creation of forms and CRUD operations with the Gii tool. If you want to write a custom code to process the form and you simply want to generate the form with all fields for the specified table, you can use the form generator tool provided by Gii.

Form Generator

This generator generates a view script file that displays a form to collect input for the specified model class.

Fields with * are required. Click on the highlighted fields to edit them.

Model Class *

User

View Name *

create

View Path *

application.views

Scenario

Code Template *

default (E:\yii\yii-1.1.11\framework\gii\generators\form\templates\default)

Preview

Enter the model's class and view name and click on the **Preview** button. You will see the same form generated by the Gii tool under the `views` folder. Click on the **Generate** button to generate the actual file.

For more information on safe attributes, visit `http://www.yiiframework.com/doc/guide/1.1/en/form.model#securing-attribute-assignments`.

For more information on validation rules, visit `http://www.yiiframework.com/doc/guide/1.1/en/form.model#declaring-validation-rules`.

Building multipage forms (Intermediate)

In this recipe, we will separate our lengthy registration form into multiple pages.

Why do we need multipage forms? Because we don't want our visitors to scroll too much and want to enable them to fill out forms as quickly as possible. Multipage forms look much shorter than a single form and fit better without much change in design; most importantly, we can group the form fields in logical sections.

Getting ready

We'll separate our existing user registration form created in the *Creating basic forms* recipe, to multipage forms. The sections will be for personal information, address details, and contact information.

How to do it...

1. All code related to the form is written in a file named _form under `protected/views/user`.

2. We are dividing the input fields into three sections, so create three separate files in the same folder with the names _page1, _page2, and _page3. Separate the code's respective files. Some sample lines are as follows:

```php
<?php $form=$this->beginWidget('CActiveForm', array(
  'id'=>'user-form',
  'enableAjaxValidation'=>false,
  'stateful'=>true,
)); ?>

<div class="row">
  <?php echo $form->labelEx($model,'first_name'); ?>
  <?php echo $form->textField($model,'first_name',
  array(
    'size'=>50,
```

```php
      'maxlength'=>50
    )); ?>
    <?php echo $form->error($model,'first_name'); ?>
  </div>
  .....
  .....
  <div class="row buttons">
    <?php echo CHtml::submitButton('Next', array(
      'name'=>'page2'
    )); ?>
  </div>
  <?php $this->endWidget(); ?>
  ....
  <div class="row buttons">
    <?php echo CHtml::submitButton('back', array(
      'name'=>'page1'
    )); ?>
    <?php echo CHtml::submitButton('Next', array(
    'name'=>'page3'
    )); ?>
  </div>

  <div class="row buttons">
    <?php echo CHtml::submitButton('Back', array(
      'name'=>'page2'
    )); ?>
    <?php echo CHtml::submitButton('submit', array(
      'name'=>'submit'
    )); ?>
  </div>
```

3. Now, in the User controller, change the code for `actionCreate` as follows:

```php
public function actionCreate()
  {
    if(isset($_POST['page1']))
    {
      $model = new User('page1');
      $this->checkPageState($model, $_POST['User']);
      $view = '_page1';
    }
    elseif(isset($_POST['page2']))
    {
      $model = new User('page1');
      $this->checkPageState($model, $_POST['User']);
```

```
      if($model->validate())
      {
        $view = '_page2';
        $model->scenario = 'page2';
      }
      else
      {
        $view = '_page1';
      }
   }

   ....

   $this->render($view, array('model'=>$model));
}
```

4. And add a function, `checkPageState()`, as follows:

```
private function checkPageState(&$model, $data)
{
  $model->attributes = $this->getPageState('page',
  array());
  $model->attributes = $data;
  $this->setPageState('page', $model->attributes);
}
```

5. Lastly, create scenarios in the model `User` to validate each page of the form separately. Add three arrays specifying all the required fields per page, as follows:

```
return array(
  array('first_name, last_name, gender, dob',
    'required', 'on'=>'page1'
  ),
  array('address_1, city, state, country',
    'required', 'on'=>'page2'
  ),
  array('phone_number_1, email_1',
    'required', 'on'=>'page3'
  ),
```

How it works...

We have separated all our input fields into three forms. Each page contains an entire standalone form that accepts the input from the user, validates it from the server, and stores the data till we finally submit this form. The parameter `stateful` passed to the `CactiveForm` widget specifies the form needed to maintain the state across the pages. To do this, Yii creates a hidden field in each form with the name `YII_PAGE_STATE`, as shown in the following screenshot:

```
▼ <div class="form">
  ▼ <form id="user-form" action="/others/sampleapp/index.php?r=user/create" method="post">
    ▼ <div style="display:none">
        <input type="hidden" name="YII_PAGE_STATE" value>
      </div>
    ▶ <p class="note">…</p>
```

All the data submitted on the first page is stored in this hidden field and passed to the server with the second page.

To read the data from this field we have used the method `getPageState()`, and to write we have used `setPageState()`. We have added a private method `checkPageState()` to the `User` controller, which reads the page state, if any, and assigns it to `$model->attributes`, then assigns data from the current form using `$model->attributes = $_POST['User']`, and finally overwrites the page state with freshly combined data.

When we click on **Next** on _page1, we set the POST variable page2, which in turn executes the second block in the `if-else` ladder in `actionCreate`. In this recipe, we create an instance of the model `User` with `scenario` set to _page1 (as we need to validate the data received from _page1). With a call to `checkPageState()`, we check the current page state and add any new data from _page1 to the page state.

Then we check if the data filled is valid using `$model->validate()`. If the model passes the validation we set, apply `view` to _page2 and set `$model->scenario` to _page2, to mark the required fields on _page2. If the validation fails, we set the view to _page1 with the validation errors set in the model.

At the end of the action, we render the selected view with the current state of the model. If any validation errors are set, they are listed on the same page; else, the next page will be rendered. The same steps are repeated for `_page2` as well.

When the **submit** button is clicked on on `_page3`, we retrieve the previous data from the page state using `getPageState()`. Here we are not using `checkPageState()` as now we do not need to store any data to the page state. We simply assign the data from `_page3` to the model, and if the model validates we save all the data to the database with `$model->save()`. After saving, we are redirected to `actionView()`, where data from all three forms is listed as shown in the following screenshot:

View User #4

ID	4
First Name	John
Last Name	Mcclane
Gender	male
Dob	1980-10-12
Address 1	Die Hard
Address 2	
City	New York City
State	New York
Country	United States
Phone Number 1	1234567890
Phone Number 2	
Email 1	John.Mcclane@diehard.com
Email 2	
Created	2013-03-18 18:46:00
Modified	0000-00-00 00:00:00

Validating forms (Intermediate)

In this recipe we will look at the data-validation options provided by Yii.

Getting ready

We'll use the form we developed in the *Building multipage forms* recipe.

How to do it...

We have fields such as **First Name**, **Last Name**, **Gender**, **Dob** (date of birth), **Phone Number 1**, **Phone Number 2**, **Email 1**, and **Email 2**. Let's add data validation for these fields. **First name** and **Last Name** will be text-only fields, **Gender** will either be **male** or **female**, and **Dob** will be a date string.

Open a User model from the `protected/models` folder. Look for the function named `rules()`. Following are the rules created for the *Building multipage forms* recipe:

```
public function rules()
{
  return array(
    array('first_name, last_name, gender, dob',
      'required', 'on'=>'page1'
  ),
  array('address_1, city, state, country',
    'required', 'on'=>'page2'
  ),
  array('phone_number_1, email_1',
    'required', 'on'=>'page3'
  ),
  array('first_name, last_name, city, state, country,
    phone_number_1, phone_number_2',
    'length', 'max'=>50
  ),
  array('gender', 'length', 'max'=>6),
  array('address_1, address_2, email_1, email_2',
    'length', 'max'=>255
  ),
  array('modified, dob', 'safe'),
  array('first_name, last_name, gender, dob,
    address_1, address_2, city, state,
    country, phone_number_1, phone_number_2, email_1,
    email_2, created, modified',
    'safe', 'on'=>'search'
  ),
}
```

This function defines the validation rules used by the Yii forms. The Gii tool has already created some simple rules by reading the definition of the user table structure. For example, the maximum length for name, **City**, **State**, and so on is 50. The field's **First Name**, **Last Name**, **Gender**, **Dob**, **Address 1**, **Address 2**, and so on are the fields required while submitting the form. Let's customise the rules as per our requirements.

1. To generate the `first_name`, `last_name`, `city`, and `state` name strings:

   ```
   array('first_name, last_name, city, state, country',
     'type', 'type'=>'string'
   ),
   ```

2. To make phone numbers numeric, add the following line to the rules array:

   ```
   array('phone_number_1, phone_number_2', 'numeric'),
   ```

3. To check if the e-mail address is a valid address, use this:

   ```
   array('email_1, email_2', 'email'),
   ```

4. To limit the values for gender, use this:

   ```
   array('gender','in','range'=>array('male','female'),
     'allowEmpty'=>false
   ),
   ```

5. To check **Dob** (date of birth) for a valid date:

   ```
   array('dob', 'date', 'format'=>'mm-dd-yyyy'),
   ```

Yii provides a range of validation options. For example:

- `boolean`: It checks for Boolean values; that is, `true(1)` or `false(0)`
- `compare`: It compares the values against the given constant
- `captcha`: For captcha code validation
- `default`: To set the default values if the field is empty
- `file`: To check the uploaded file's type, size, and number of files

There are many other options too.

How it works...

The `rules()` function returns a set of rules in a main array, with each rule specified in its separate array for one or more attributes. These rules are used by the `validate()` method of a model to determine validation of data on the server side. The `save()` method internally calls this validation and requires it to succeed before saving the record.

For client-side validation, Yii sends additional JavaScript with page contents that contain validation rules coded in JavaScript. With the following code, we can set the trigger to call client-side validation:

```php
<?php $form=$this->beginWidget('CActiveForm', array(
  'id'=>'user-form',
  'enableAjaxValidation'=>false,
  'clientOptions'=>array(
    'validateOnSubmit'=>true,
    'validateOnChange'=>true,
  ),
```

The `validateOnSubmit` method calls the client-side form field validation before actually submitting a form (on the click of a submit button), while `validateOnChange` triggers field validation on the `onchange` event of the respective field.

There's more...

You can visit the following website for various validation rules:

- `http://www.yiiframework.com/wiki/56/`
- `http://www.yiiframework.com/wiki/168/create-your-own-validation-rule/`
- `http://www.yiiframework.com/wiki/266/understanding-scenarios/`

AJAX forms (Advanced)

Yii provides some useful AJAX-based options to make your forms more responsive and interactive. You can set Yii forms to validate fields on change and/or on form submission. This validation is performed by an AJAX call to the server validating the input fields without refreshing the page.

In this recipe we will learn how to enable AJAX support for form validations and submissions.

Getting ready

To see this in action, we will use the simple form generated in the *Creating basic forms* recipe.

How to do it...

1. Open the file `/protected/views/user/_form.php`.

2. To enable AJAX-based server-side validation, change the property `enableAjaxValidation` to `true` with the following code:

```
<?php $form=$this->beginWidget('CActiveForm', array(
  'id'=>'user-form',
  'enableAjaxValidation'=>true,
)); ?>
```

3. To process AJAX validation requests, add the following lines to the action created in `UserController.php`:

```
. . .
$model=new User;
if(isset($_POST['ajax']) && $_POST['ajax']==='user-form')
{
  echo CActiveForm::validate($model);
  Yii::app()->end();
}
if(isset($_POST['User']))
. . .
```

With this, we have enabled AJAX-based server-side validation for our form.

How it works...

When we set `enableAjaxValidation` to true, Yii automatically adds some JavaScript code to our form page. This code tracks the changes in the form fields and sends a request to the server to validate the changes. We can set the separate URL for validating the form data; by default, the validation requests are submitted to the `action` attribute of the form. In our case it is the same `actionCreate` attribute that is used to render the form.

In `actionCreate`, we have added some code to check for AJAX validation requests. If we receive an AJAX request, we simply call the `CActiveForm::validate($model)` method to validate the data. This method returns the validation results in JSON form, which is then passed to the client browser.

If the respective fields are valid, they will be marked with CSS for denoting class success (green color by default); else, it gets marked with red color for class error and the error description is displayed below the respective field as well as in the error-summary section.

The problem with `enableAjaxValidation` is that it sends validation requests for changes in any of the form fields, by default. This creates lot of traffic on the server.

To reduce server traffic with AJAX requests, add the following lines to the form definition:

```php
<?php $form=$this->beginWidget('CActiveForm', array(
  'id'=>'user-form',
  'enableAjaxValidation'=>true,
  'clientOptions'=>array(
    'validateOnSubmit'=>true,
    'validateOnChange'=>false,
  ),
)); ?>
```

With this line, we have disabled the validation requests on field-change events and enabled AJAX-based validations on submitting the form. This avoids the individual validation requests and sends a single request before final submission of the form. If this request fails, the form submission is cancelled with the error description added to the form. After successful validation, a regular POST request is sent to the server submitting the form.

With this additional code, you get complete AJAX-based form submission:

```php
<?php $form=$this->beginWidget('CActiveForm', array(
  'id'=>'user-form',
  'enableAjaxValidation'=>true,
  'clientOptions'=>array(
    'validateOnSubmit'=>true,
    'validateOnChange'=>false,
    'afterValidate'=>'js:submitForm', //JS function
  ),
)); ?>
```

Add the following HTML code to _form.php. This will hold the result of form submission.

```html
<span id="result"></span>
```

Add the following JavaScript to _form.php under protected/views/user:

```html
<script type="text/javascript">
function submitForm (form, data, hasError){
  //check for validation errors
  if (!hasError){
    var url = form.attr('action');
    $.post(url, form.serialize(), function(res){
      $('#result').html(res);
    });
  }
  // return false to avoid traditional form submit
  return false;
}
</script>
```

Set some additional code in the `actionCreate` method of `UserController`, as follows:

```
if(isset($_POST['ajax']) && $_POST['ajax']==='user-form')
{
  echo CActiveForm::validate($model);
  Yii::app()->end();
}

if(Yii::app()->request->isAjaxRequest)
{
  //do stuff like validate or save model
  //and set message accordingly
  echo 'Registration successful!!';
  Yii::app()->end();
}
```

What we did is set the forms `afterValidate` to submit AJAX request to `actionCreate()`. As we are not setting `$_POST['ajax']`, we track this event with `Yii::app()->request->isAjaxRequest`. If it's an AJAX request, simply save the model and return the success message. This is then displayed in the `span` tag on the form page.

Notice that we have set the `submitForm` function to always return `false` to avoid the traditional non-AJAX form submission.

There's more...

Additionally, Yii provides three static methods.

- `CHTML::ajaxLink()`
- `CHTML::ajaxButton()`
- `CHTML::ajaxSubmitButton()`

These methods automatically create the respective HTML elements and additionally add the jQuery code for AJAX-based requests/response handling.

The following lines demonstrate the use of AJAX using these helpers:

```
echo CHtml::ajaxLink(
  'Submit',
  array('user/view', 'id' => $id), // Yii URL
  array('update' => '#result') // jQuery selector
);
```

This will create an HTML link element with the name `Submit`. On clicking this link, a request is posted to `actionView` of `UserController`. The first parameter provides a name or text to be used for the link. The second parameter specifies its target or `href` attribute. The third parameter specifies the AJAX option update that is set to replace the contents of the HTML element `#result`.

You can process the response data on the client script with following callback function:

```
echo CHtml::ajaxLink(
  'Submit',
  array('user/view', 'id' => $id),
  array(
    'dataType'=>'json',
    'success' => 'js:function(data){
      console.log(data);
      alert(data.msg); //message element in response
    }'),
);
```

You can find more information on AJAX forms at the following links:

▶ http://www.yiiframework.com/wiki/394/javascript-and-ajax-with-yii/

▶ http://www.yiiframework.com/doc/api/1.1/CActiveForm#clientOptions-detail

Uploading files (Advanced)

Let's add the upload functionality to our registration form. We'll add a file-upload dialog, asking the user to upload his image.

Getting ready

We'll use the form we have developed in the *Creating basic forms* recipe.

How to do it...

1. Let's start with editing our model `User.php`. Add a public attribute named `$image`.

   ```
   public $image;

   public static function model($className=__CLASS__)
   {
     return parent::model($className);
   }
   ```

2. Now add some validation rules for this attribute.

```
return array(
  array('image', 'file', 'allowEmpty' => true,
    'types' => 'jpg, jpeg, gif, png'
  ),
  ...
);
```

3. Add the attribute's name to this attribute:

```
'image'=>'Upload Photo',
```

4. Edit _form.php under `protected/views/user` to add the following lines to enable this form to accept file uploads:

```
'htmlOptions' => array('enctype' => 'multipart/form-data'),
<code in uploads/_form.php>
```

5. Finally, add the following lines to the `UserController.php` action created, to save the uploaded file:

```
if(isset($_POST['User']))
{
  $model->attributes=$_POST['User'];
  $model->image=CUploadedFile::getInstance($model,'image');
  if($model->save())
  {
    $path=Yii::getPathOfAlias(
    'webroot.images.'.$model->first_name
    );
    $model->image->saveAs($path);
    $this->redirect(array('view','id'=>$model->id));
  }
}
```

That's it, we are done. Now try to fill the form, select the file to be uploaded and you can find the uploaded file at the `web_root/images` folder.

How it works...

At the start, we set a public attribute to our `User` model to hold the file data. Next we set some validation rules to specify that the file upload is not compulsory and the user can upload only `.jpg`, `.gif`, and `.png` files.

Then we set our form to accept file uploads. As we are uploading the binary data in the form of a file, we need to enable our form to accept binary data. We did this with `'enctype' =>` `'multipart/form-data'`. Additionally, the form method must be set to `POST`.

At this stage we are done with the upload part, but at the server side we need some logic to process the uploaded contents. We added this functionality with the following line:

```
$model->image=CUploadedFile::getInstance($model,'image');
```

To get the uploaded contents in `$model->image`, we add the following line:

```
$model->image->saveAs($path.$model->first_name);
```

We have saved and received data in a file with the same name as the user's first name. Alternatively, you can get the original filename with `$model->image->getName()`.

We have used two components provided by Yii. Following are the two components:

- ▸ CUploadedFile: This represents the information for an uploaded file. It's a wrapper class for the `$_FILE` array that PHP uses to hold uploaded files. We have used its `getInstance()` method to get the uploaded file and then used `saveAs()` to save the data to the file. Additionally, we can get other information about the file, including the name, temporary name, type, size, and errors. Get more details on the website `http://www.yiiframework.com/doc/api/1.1/CUploadedFile`.

- ▸ CFileValidator: This verifies if an attribute is receiving a valid uploaded file. With the file validator, we can make the `file` field compulsory, specify the maximum number of files, and specify the minimum and maximum limits on the file size and a file type. We can also set the details of the errors to be displayed. By adding the following lines in the `rules` array of the model, we can enable the `file` field validation:

```
return array(
  array('image', 'file', 'allowEmpty' => true,
    'types' => 'jpg, jpeg, gif, png'
  ),
  . . .
);
```

With these lines, we have set the `image` attribute to be optional and we have restricted the file types to image files.

You can get more details from the website `http://www.yiiframework.com/doc/api/1.1/CFileValidator/`.

Using multiple models (Intermediate)

This recipe explains how to use multiple models within a single form.

Getting ready

We'll use the form we have developed in the *Building multipage forms* recipe.

Create a new table order. This will represent the orders placed by the users.

```
CREATE TABLE IF NOT EXISTS 'order' (
  'id' int(11) NOT NULL AUTO_INCREMENT,
  'user_id' int(11) NOT NULL,
  'product_name' varchar(255) NOT NULL,
  'quantity' int(11) NOT NULL,
  PRIMARY KEY ('id'),
  KEY 'user_id' ('user_id')
) ENGINE=InnoDB DEFAULT CHARSET=latin1 AUTO_INCREMENT=1 ;
```

Create a model for this table using the Gii tool.

How to do it...

Let's add this new model to the `actionCreate` method developed for multiple forms. We will need to add one more step/page to the action as follows:

```
...
$this->checkPageState($model, Yii::app()->request->getPost('User',
array()));
$this->setPageState('order', Yii::app()->request->getPost('
Order', array()));

...
...
if($model->validate())
{
  $view = '_page4';
  $order = new Order();
  $order->attributes = $this->getPageState(
    'order', array()
  );
}

...

else if(isset($_POST['submit']))
```

```
{
  $model = new User('page3');
  $order = new Order();
  $model->attributes = $this->getPageState(
    'page', array()
  );
  $order->attributes = $_POST['Order'];
  if($model->validate())
  {
    $model->save();
    $order->user_id = $model->id;
    if($order->validate())
    {
      $order->save();
      $this->redirect(array('view', 'id'=>$model->id));
    }
  }
  $view = '_page4';
}
```

Next, create a view for _page4.

```
...
<div class="row">
  <?php echo $form->labelEx($order,'product_name'); ?>
  <?php echo $form->textField($order,'product_name'); ?>
  <?php echo $form->error($order,'product_name'); ?>
</div>
<div class="row">
  <?php echo $form->labelEx($order,'quantity'); ?>
  <?php echo $form->numberField ($order,'quantity'); ?>
  <?php echo $form->error($order,'quantity'); ?>
</div>
<div class="row buttons">
  <?php echo CHtml::submitButton('Back', array(
    'name'=>'page3')); ?>
  <?php echo CHtml::submitButton('submit', array(
    'name'=>'submit')); ?>
</div>
...
```

Change the **submit** button in the view of _page3 to the following:

```
<?php echo CHtml::submitButton('Next', array(
  'name'=>'page4'
)); ?>
```

We are done; try the new form in your browser. It will look something like the following screenshot:

How it works...

We introduced an order model in the fourth page of our multipage form with the following code:

```
if ($model->validate())
{
  $view = '_page4';
  $order = new Order();
  $order->attributes = $this->getPageState('order', array());
}
```

First we check if the data we received in the third step for the model `User` is valid. If the model validates, we set our view page to `_page4`. Then we create a new model named `Order`. On the third line, we simply check if there's any saved state for the model `Order`; this is useful if the user moves back after filling the data of `Order`.

In the same way, we have added some code in the third step to check if the user has moved back from `_page4` after filling the form fields. So we save the current state of `_page4`. Notice the use of `Yii::app()->request->getPost('User', array())` line of code. The `getPost()` method is used to get the named `POST` value. The first parameter is the name of the `POST` field and the second parameter is the default value if the `POST` field with the given name is not set. Similarly, you can use the `getParam()` method to get the parameters of `GET`.

Next, in the final step, we assign the saved state to the `User` model, and `$_POST` data to the `Order` model. As we have already loaded a save state on the page, `$_POST` will hold the updated data (if any) or the data in that saved state.

Then we validate the `User` model with `if ($model->validate())`. After successful validation, we save the `User` model and assign the user's ID to the `Order` model with `$order->user_id = $model->id`. Then we save the `Order` model too. If it's successful, we redirect to view the page; else, we redirect to the fourth page to solve the form errors.

There's more...

We could use the transactional feature of the database while storing the data; that is, if the saving of the order model fails, we could discard the User model entirely by rolling back the transaction as follows:

```
if($model->validate())
{
    $transaction = Yii::app()->db->beginTransaction();
    try
    {
        $model->save();
        $order->user_id = $model->id;
        if(!$order-> save())
            throw new Exception('Order data invalid');
        $transaction->commit();
        $this->redirect(array('view', 'id'=>$model->id));
    }
    catch(Exception e)
    {
        $transaction->rollBack();
        $view = 'page4';
    }
}
```

For more details on database transaction visit the website `en.wikipedia.org/wiki/Database_transaction`.

Transactional queries support in Yii can be looked up on the website `http://www.yiiframework.com/doc/guide/1.1/en/database.dao#using-transactions`.

Customizing looks (Advanced)

In this recipe we will look at the various options to customize the look of page elements. Yii provides attributes such as `htmlOptions`, `labelOptions`, and `cssFile` to add your own CSS rules to the page elements.

How to do it...

1. Use your own class for the form as follows:

```
$form=$this->beginWidget('CActiveForm', array(
    'id'=>'user-form',
    'htmlOptions' => array('class' => 'myclass'),
));
```

2. Set the HTML options (name, ID, class, and so on) for elements as follows:

```
$htmlOptions = array('class'=>'myClass', 'id'=>'myId')
$form->textField($model, $attribute, $htmlOptions)
```

Using Skins, we can proceed as follows:

1. Enable Skins in the application configuration with the following code:

```
'widgetFactory'=>array(
  'class'=>'CWidgetFactory',
  'enableSkin'=>true,
)
```

2. To create a new skin for a widget, create a file with the name of the widget in the Skins folder, that is, `/protected/views/skins/CDetailView.php`, with the following code:

```
return array(
  'default'=>array(
    'htmlOptions'=>array(
      'class'=>'class_1',
    ),
    'template'=>'<span>{label}</span><span>{value}</span>',
  ),
  'stripped'=>array(
    'htmlOptions'=>array(
      'class'=>'stripped',
    ),
    'template'=>'<span>{label}</span><span>{value}</span>',
  )
);
```

3. Use the widget with a Skin.

4. Use a default skin.

```
$this->widget('CDetailView);
```

5. Or, use our created Skin as follows:

```
$this->widget('CDetailView, array('skin'=>'stripped'));
```

How it works...

We can change the default CSS rules applied to the form elements with the parameter `htmlOptions`. Here we can specify a custom CSS class or provide inline styling rules as follows:

```
$htmlOptions => array('attribute' => 'value');
$form->textField($model, $attribute, $htmlOptions);
$form->dropDownList($model, $attribute, $data, $htmlOptions);
```

In the same way, elements such as `textfield` and `dropdownlist` and the label `radioButtonsLists` provide an optional parameter `$htmlOptions` to customize the look of a given element.

If all forms across your application are supposed to use the same styling rules, instead of repeating `htmlOptions` for each form, you can add these rules to `widgetFactory` in the application configuration. In `protected/config/main.php`, add the following lines:

```
...
'components'=>array(
  'widgetFactory'=>array(
    'class'=>'CWidgetFactory',
    'widgets'=>array(
      'CActiveForm'=>array(
        'htmlOptions'=>array(
          'class'=>'myClass1 myClass2',
        ),
      ),
    ),
  )
...
)
```

Now you can specify the element with the following:

```
$form=$this->beginWidget('CActiveForm', array(
    'id'=>'user-form',
));
```

If you want some forms to use different CSS rules than the ones specified in `widgetFactory`, you can do it by specifying the `htmlOptions` array for this form. Additionally, you can customize form styles with the following `clientOption` attributes:

```
$form=$this->beginWidget('CActiveForm', array(
  'clientOptions'=>array(
    'errorCssClass'=>'errorClass',
    'successCssClass'=>'successClass',
    'validatingCssClass'=>'inProgress',
    'errorMessageCssClass'=>'msgClass',
)));
```

These attributes are explained as follows:

▸ The `errorCssClass` attribute allows you to set the CSS class to be assigned to the container whose associated input has the AJAX validation error

▸ With the `successCssClass` attribute, you can set the class for the container whose associated input passes AJAX validation

▸ The `validatingCssClass` attribute allows you to set the CSS class to be assigned to the container whose associated input is currently being validated via AJAX

▸ The `errorMessageCssClass` attribute sets the CSS class to the error message returned by AJAX validation

▸ You can also change the container element for an input field with the `inputContainer` attribute

For widgets such as `detailView`, `gridView`, and `listView`, you can specify the template to be used to change the way these widgets are rendered.

```
$this->widget('zii.widgets.CDetailView', array(
  'htmlOptions'=>array( 'class'=>'myClass'),
  'template'=>'<span>{label}</span><span>{value}</span>',
  . . .
));
```

We can use Skins to customise the look of Yii widgets; all the rules we specified under `widgetFactory` in `main.php` can be moved to the Skin files. Additionally, we can specify multiple Skins for each widget and decide which Skin to use when we need it. When the `enableSkin` option for `widgetFactory` is set to `true`, Yii will try to find the Skins before rendering the widgets. If the Skins are not available, Yii's inbuilt styling will be used.

There's more...

You can find more details on customizing Yii widgets on the link `http://danaluther.blogspot.in/2012/02/leveraging-widgets-widget-factory-and.html`.

Thank you for buying
Instant Building Multi-Page Forms with Yii How-to

About Packt Publishing

Packt, pronounced 'packed', published its first book "*Mastering phpMyAdmin for Effective MySQL Management*" in April 2004 and subsequently continued to specialize in publishing highly focused books on specific technologies and solutions.

Our books and publications share the experiences of your fellow IT professionals in adapting and customizing today's systems, applications, and frameworks. Our solution based books give you the knowledge and power to customize the software and technologies you're using to get the job done. Packt books are more specific and less general than the IT books you have seen in the past. Our unique business model allows us to bring you more focused information, giving you more of what you need to know, and less of what you don't.

Packt is a modern, yet unique publishing company, which focuses on producing quality, cutting-edge books for communities of developers, administrators, and newbies alike. For more information, please visit our website: www.packtpub.com.

Writing for Packt

We welcome all inquiries from people who are interested in authoring. Book proposals should be sent to author@packtpub.com. If your book idea is still at an early stage and you would like to discuss it first before writing a formal book proposal, contact us; one of our commissioning editors will get in touch with you.

We're not just looking for published authors; if you have strong technical skills but no writing experience, our experienced editors can help you develop a writing career, or simply get some additional reward for your expertise.

Yii Rapid Application Development Hotshot

ISBN: 978-1-84951-750-8   Paperback: 340 pages

Become a RAD hotshop with YII, the world's most popular PHP framework

1. A series of projects to help you learn Yii and Rapid Application Development

2. Learn how to build and incorporate key web technologies

3. Use as a cookbook to look up key concepts, or work on the projects from start to finish for a complete web application

Agile Web Application Development with Yii1.1 and PHP5

ISBN: 978-1-84719-958-4   Paperback: 368 pages

Fast-track your web application development: by harnessing the power of the Yii PHP Framework

1. A step-by-step guide to creating a modern, sophisticated web application using an incremental and iterative approach to software development

2. Build a real-world, user-based, database-driven project task management application using the Yii development framework

3. Take a test-driven design (TDD) approach to software development utilizing the Yii testing framework

Please check **www.PacktPub.com** for information on our titles

www.ingramcontent.com/pod-product-compliance
Lightning Source LLC
Chambersburg PA
CBHW060444060326
40690CB00019B/4325